QUE

TIM REYNOLDS

QUE

Halty Ferguson
Cambridge
1971

First edition

ISBN 0-912604-05-0   L. C. Card No. 76-155304

Paperback cover design by Michael McCurdy

Some of these sequences & sections first appeared in *El Corno Emplumado, Fire Escape, From a Window, Miscellaneous Man, Noose, Riata, Stony Brook, Inner Space,* SLOCUM (Unicorn Press, 1967), and the Phoenix Book Shop Oblong Octavo Series.

CONTENTS

Para los 81 compañeros
del Campo Militar #2,
& for Don Greer in Huntsville:

Algún día quemaremos todo esto.

abrirse   ¡pero cómo!

Isabel Fraire

"Answer as there is to all
unask" & stopped
there. Is it after all you I can't be? Look,
there are letters &

poems, & we
aren't letters, Lynne.

                              Your
light's off, but look, no, only
Andromeda, blurry

thumbprint these December
nights. &
that mother's a right
smart piece, & moving

out.   & not poems

Ann Arbor, 12.66

1. Carnaval

1.

What was I
there, then, or
who, or among whom, or
was I? In that storm of masks &

mariachis & fuegos artificiales, yo
ya no fui yo ni mi casa
tu casa.

               Maricones,
machismo's

flip side, canter, & among these snows
of falling burnings still
always & always
masked a fist-sized moon

2.

CAYÓ, over my café
con leche, COMO
METEORO. He'll
rate a crater on the dark side

anyhow. Earle
a pockhole?
No.
      FALLÓ
EL PARACAÍDAS, ours

too somewhere, I fall &
fall, we
fall, Lu-
cretius, where is thy Swerve?

3. *for John*

This stillness of things
falling   .   I clasp its knees, its
beard :   Do not
kill me. But nothing I can say,

do, drowns that

silence when the V-2 cuts
out, that silence of fires
falling the ai-yip-yips &
marimbas counter-

point.   It

loves me not, floats
no manly
compassion down, as :
Patroklos, your better, died :

or   :   me, me, me, me, me

4.

Dee Duerson & the
boy in the blue
sweater, Judson, Avril, Ellen
& who else have I

betrayed today?

Mary K,
of course, &
Anthony, & Bob
& Sam & Vivian & Janet &

Bill. Lynne. Hannah. The

usual crowd, no end
to these redheads in turquoise
sweaters   .
                    & I is a
watchbird watching

us: & who have *you* screwed today?

5.

¡PAREN! ME GUÍAN
MAL, ¿NO
COMPRENDEN?

They're sluicing confetti

down the Portal sewers.
My cuffs are full.
       & one enormous
ash drifted, last
night, through my window, from some

fire in the sky.
       Carnaval

itself was tired, you could
feel it. Feel it. Stop it. It's going
wrong, can't you

understand?

6. *para* Οὖτις

Done. Booms, radiances

fall, face falls
away, dwindling back black corridors
of hell home, where you learned
survival : when the blind

matador lumbers close, you scream: 'I'm Nobody!
Nobody!'
                    Only, viajera tan

perseverante, that
I loved you when I saw you
shipwrecked, eyes
ensimismados, cloudy with other cities &

islands, some
horrible. That, & you were gone again, tacking home

forever.
                    I
cried for you just now, &
for Earle, myself, Komarov, sailor who wore your
simple skin so proudly.
                    Carnaval's

done.
            Nobody home.   Nobody

Veracruz, 4.67

2. Kaleidoscope

para Isabel,
que me regala un caleidoscopio

1.

'Donde se cruzan dos
calles cuatro
cantinas', where
we passed, '56, strangeness

to me te
tuteando in mud, brick &
rut. To
say what? Te

quiero, Isabel,
whatever
wilderness of mirrors that
puts us in, all what's

real, but changed

2.

Time

        taken time
        given, an
        exchange, can-
        tina, Calle

        de Mina : Twist

        y gritos, La vi
        allá, No puedo comprar mi
        amor, Ella te ama, time
                      gone &

changed in that going   .
                It was all there

        always, with Desmond in the Oxford

Grille ('s always there)
that misery I can't
scratch : but
              Driving back from New
Hampshire with liquor I pulled over, to

listen : I want to hold your hand

3.

Haunts your closed face some
Toltec father's
deathbound profile, alien
as Teotihuacan's godborn

geometry, core-
cold still in all that spill
of sun, a
waterfall of shining children down the

Pyramid of the Moon, your closed
face, whose
strangeness
bewilders me — open your

eyes, *your* eyes

4.

hemos derrocado a un tirano después de años de lucha,
vamos a realizar la más grande revolución de este siglo,
este país será transformado de una manera que usted no imagina,
todo eso hemos hecho y vamos a hacer y usted viene de México
   a preguntar cuándo nos quitamos las barbas

                    —El Ché, a un corresponsal, 1.6.59

Bearded ghost, everywhere,
nowhere, spirit
over the waters, in the air, on the
streets of Haiphong, La Paz, Detroit (I

felt your passing at

Antioch, San
Francisco, Watts — the man at the corner
with his son, that gesture: remember,
it was *us* did this — but hardly

understood), ghost haunted by

fusilados, sombra, hombre, some-
where, how, you
share this Orion we're under, help us help it
come, for David, Rolando, Anthony,

                    Ché, no,
                    don't shave

5.

it's some way of seeing I chase across a time
     of linked spaces
         chased by shining & harassing eyes
         time is water lapsing through fingers
you are my flesh
     no one else watches me
         with those eyes of a lost owl
         eyes that put names to things &
             strip names from things
I fall unsouled down some well where colors whirl
         float in a soft shining
your hands hold me up without touching me
things' souls turn toward me
with the key I've taken from the dark casebox of your heart
     I unlock words
     & they drop down over things
     & fold about them
         own as their skins

*(after Isabel Fraire, "persigo una mirada",
in* Revista de Bellas Artes, *mayo / junio '66)*

6.

Nothing
smaller than a real world
to hold our heads full of worlds —
everything, everything,

young whores in
Osaka chanting after me *Barū
mūn, yu sa mi standīn arōn*, beer-
stench & endless rain in

Monterrey, our
loves, our children, our
memories of hell, terror, light, stranger,
light where these dark

lives cross

México DF, 7.67

3. Oz

1.

Toto, I have a feeling we're not in
Kansas any more

Not prosthetic, an
extension — a
completion :   'Accidentally, I
focused the tube on a dark blue spot

in the sky

between the stars' —
that *rest* of us, in
Andromeda maybe, the leg buried on
Guam.

It hung by one

flank from her flank,

checked red & yellow suit, string
tie, dust in the
creases of its doll's patent leather
shoes & face,

tiny, grey, wise, dead

2.

   . . . Oil. Can . . .

'Up in the dark
like monks, carried our bombsights
to briefing, then out to the planes,
all in the dark.

Warmed up, took off,

climbed, broke
cloud, man, & thousands of
B-52's crystallizing in formation,
fighters swarming around like

flies, man, sun whanging off

metal, first light that world's day
ours, & the word comes through static &
we synchronize for Dresden
                            & you asleep stateside
in the night, seven maybe, you & your fucking

Poetry, flat as piss on a plate

3.

. . . a star named Kansas . . .

To whatever
circle, so many
tangents — Pollak, Milosz,
Slonimsky, an old man I saw

crying, & the V-
2's, the silence of no
phone but   :   Give me to stand
I'll move the earth
                                No

where to
run, friends, no
place to stand
                    & the wind

spins fearful circles in the sand

4. *In Memoriam : Otis Redding*

Is he good or is he wicked?
Very good, but very mysterious

My grandfather,
curiously enough, drowned
in that same lake, Monona, hanging
for hours to a tipped canoe with I A

Richards — still living, curiously
enough. & just now a burglar woke me, only
a shape at the open
door like a cutout in the cops'

basement. He woke me from a dream
of your black bones dancing
with my grandfather's white bones, deep
down there where it's all black anyway.

I called (Hey, man)
                but he was gone,
                        out the back gate

5. *In Memoriam : El Ché*

> *This is a day of liberation for all the*
> *Munchkins and their descendants. If any.*

Late

        October & the god is

        dead again, root

        tassel &

ear of our resurrection,

        & we

        agonize again with the god

        whose gifts are agony & hope

Come March we'll

        dance your rising

        as we howl your fall now

        in January's icy center we'll

remember who's under our bootsoles

6.

O wear my gingham with a difference
horizon around me like a plate
whistling without faith for a wind
O believe birdsong & smaragdine blaze

> Every morning, seven,
> in your always Oz, Erika, four,
> you woke me to play you
> Wizzer . . .   Where we've been

Yellow brick string unravelled about me
I Dorothy remember a green place

ἐν καθαρῷ

("in an open space" — Alice's daddy — "a space
free of dead bodies") weep among my faithful Zoas

Brainless   Gutless   Heartless   Homeless

4.

1.

To bind you
in, you
names, you hands, to
have you

birdtorn 4 A
M's
I'm
with no one I

love, to have you
bound, you I
love, & you,
you

2.

To furnish it all
myself, buy,
build from bare
beaverboard out,

pictures of my
friends on the
dresser, all
my books

signed with friends' loving
inscriptions, a table
to sit at
& a chair to sit on

3.

To only let
happen, as though
by a sum of many small
grains gathering

mass, defining
a center, a larger thing, a
weight all one relation, might
come about,

condensing, water-
bead on a cold Coors, &
find its some one shape
inside, & shine

4.

To sum up:
to make small:
to make mine:
to make do:

to bind, define,
gather, buy,
build; to make;
to find

to sit at a table,
to sit on a chair,
to do something simple
as that, made, simply,
or found, here, there

5. Clinamen

1.

& so as these endless particles rain plumb
through endless void by their own
weights borne down they at no
particular time entirely nor no
place alter vector slanting — &
from such bangings world; thus this
we may term mother of Rome & gods
& men, or
Venus, this slipping away always from
(as you may term it) fate. & never
otherwise would nature have made none.

2.   *for Flagstaff's Finest*

Folks, I give you
Arizona, tightest little asshole
in the Southwest!

>   Applause

More McCarran Act
concentration camps per
capita than
any other single state!

>   Applause

36 retired
generals & pretty near
500 colonels!

>   Applause

Let's give it a big hand, folks!

>   Prolonged

>   applause.

3.

Nor then can nothing be preserved nor
nothing destroyed nor nothing loose
nock from hard string never though
no night comes day nor day night but's
wailing with squalling mixed — we *will*
not go where we must go & always it
pains us. & so we must love it. Or not?
Bronze like ice
dwindles in this brutal light. & us small,
& it big, why no lightning sliding across
all our sky could halve or quarter it!

4.

Because I love you so, John &
Dorothy Bradford, because
you love me not
because

of the chalky Aristotelian
devil I kill in me & he
will not die, but
anyway,

I'd write you a poem if I
could, but tonight
all I have are
words,

these

5.

Nor then am I neither preserved nor
otherwise destroyed nor can follow not
one particle to its hole to find me,
yapping & snarling in my personal dark,
Ai yip yip, nor among high mountains find
no some one place from where all is
down & out, sheep & burning shepherds one
shining in a plain.
No Blake to find me no such real sun-
hammered temple, show me some cracked road
out of this bonfire, let someone else bring me down.

6.

alive even a dark
nimbus moved about you & your
            laugh fell meaninglessly as
            water over stones
your hair was rooted in a cloudless sky
your eyes

& if I see myself in
you, my
hands nerveless as kelp, in
what glass are you dissolving now, &

your name & your
face, leaving only quick gooseflesh
                    over somebody's skin,
a sudden image, senseless, caught
                        somewhere, lost

muy pronto para siempre

(after Isabel Fraire, 'aun en la vida un halo oscuro
te rodeaba', in Revista de Bellas Artes,
mayo / junio '66)

7.

They told me you were sleeping
in doorways in
Reno or
somewhere, drinking
iodine or whatever drunks drink   .

Forsan et haec olim meminisse iuvabit

you wrote in a book
you gave me
in the shop on Filmore ten
years ago (but I lost it)

You told me it meant
(laughing) : Some day
we'll remember all this crap & laugh & laugh   .

A still bay, long withdrawn, waves break
their backs on the island outside & flop sloshing
back, hanging rocks, nymph-locus, you can
see your face in the dark stillness, rising, falling

That rock-cradled calm after violence, Bill,
Bill Husk, have you found it?

8.

It comes to go & goes to come
as from rain rise shining
crops & black boughs green
& cities flower with children
& tired cows proffer fat dugs
& calves on rickety legs
stagger drunk with the milk
through grass minds blasted —
born's from gone things &
no thing otherwise born
nothing dies never only
you   you   you   you

Austin, 8.68

6. Tlatelolco

On the afternoon of 2 October, 1968, in Colonia Tlatelolco, the Díaz-Ordaz administration improved its public image for the Olympics by massacring several hundred Mexican citizens, some of them in their own living rooms. Soldiers & officers in the prison camp, none of whom had seen the entire action, estimated between three & five hundred dead; the official word, repeated by the official US press, is 31; as of July 1969 756 deaths had been verified. The firing of automatic weapons continued for more than two hours. The bodies of the dead were burned, as earlier bodies had been. Thousands remain, still, in the jails & prison camps of Mexico City.

*

The prose quotation in #2 is from Lévi-Strauss, those in #3 from Michelet.

1.

"porque
  no tengan niños", end
  of anecdote, something
  about tourists;   I

nodded, smiled, "Así es." I
can say about what, not
how, I want, understand
others not much.

Still, it's
beginning, learning
the language : & tomorrow
the aduaneros, I

think, may let me pass

Laredo, 8.68

2.

Remembering Crane, Whitman, the
crossing of water I crossed
the Rio Bravo, no
grato, not
in Mexico, by
American Airlines

gratis

The invocation accompanying the crossing
of a watercourse is divided into various
segments, corresponding respectively to
the moment when the travelers place their
feet in the water, when they move them,
when the water covers their feet entirely —

no
invocation for water
closing over heads; Pawnee streams
run shallow, our bitch of a West ocean horizonless &
grey, grey

3.

for Keith

Come at last (Livre
XXI) to this
summit of the Terror,
you encounter here only a

dry-as-dustness, no
sign of life

> The story is told that he,
> Fouquier-Tinville, wanted
> to enthrone the guillotine
> in the Tribunal itself:
> the Committee asked him
> if he'd gone mad

dry, dry as the dry
heads, dry hearts, dry fingers
endlessly scrabbling documents (Trotsky:
"Nobody could invent stuff like this"

> No matter how fast work went ahead,
> the guillotine did its job so fast that
> Picpus, overloaded, bubbling and
> fermenting, threatened to cause a
> mass exodus from the district. Not
> even the grave-diggers would go near
> it. The Commune was notified of this
> on the 8th of Thermidor and thought
> it could probably last at least another
> day or two, "so long as thyme, sage and
> juniper were burned on the spot"

Archivist, I

record of the Terror only
its desiccation, how dry I am

4.

Avalanche of birdsong dwindled
to these few
pebbles

                piu   piu

The dawn stars roll over &
over, occurring beyond
understanding or manipulation, beyond
belief, beyond
denial. Accept us we
must. Almost
a third of a century, I
begin finally to be-
lieve in history

                      Que   Que

                              What

              does it mean

                        What

          did it ever mean

                  Austin, 7.69

THIS FIRST EDITION OF *QUE* IS LIMITED TO
1000 COPIES BOUND IN PAPER, PRINTED ON
MOHAWK SUPERFINE, AND 150 NUMBERED
COPIES SIGNED BY THE AUTHOR, PRINTED
ON FABRIANO TEXT AND BOUND IN FULL
LINEN BY WILLIAM FERGUSON. THE TYPE IS
HERMANN ZAPF'S PALATINO. HAND-SET
AND PRINTED AT THE FERGUSON PRESS,
CAMBRIDGE, MASSACHUSETTS, JULY 1971

RL